A HANDCART PIONEER

MARY ANN HAFEN
Taken in 1931, at the age of seventy-seven

RECOLLECTIONS OF
A HANDCART PIONEER
OF 1860

A Woman's Life
on the Mormon Frontier

By

MARY ANN HAFEN

University of Nebraska Press
Lincoln and London

Manufactured in the United States of America.

First Bison Book printing: May 1983
Most recent printing indicated by the first digit below:
    3   4   5   6   7   8   9   10

Library of Congress Cataloging in Publication Data

Hafen, Mary Ann, 1854–
   Recollections of a handcart pioneer of 1860.

   Reprint. Originally published: Denver, Colo. : Priv.
print., 1938.
   1. Hafen, Mary Ann, 1854–   . 2. Frontier and
pioneer life—Utah. 3. Frontier and pioneer life—Nevada.
4. Utah—Social life and customs. 5. Nevada—Social life
and customs. 6. Mormons—Utah—Biography. 7. Mormons—
Nevada—Biography. 8. Utah—Biography. 9. Nevada—Biography. I. Title.
F826.H14 1983   979.2'02'0924 [B]   82-23868
ISBN 0-8032-2325-0
ISBN 0-8032-7219-7 (pbk.)

Reprinted from the privately printed first edition (1938), omitting
Appendix B, Family Record.

A HANDCART PIONEER

FOREWORD

My children and grandchildren have for some years urged me to write something of my experiences, so I have tried to comply by giving the following sketch of my life. Having been reared under pioneer conditions, with little opportunity for schooling, I felt unequal to the task, but have humbly done my best. My son, Roy, his wife, Ann, and my granddaughter, Juanita, have assisted with the writing by asking me questions to bring out more information and details. Roy has attended to the publication. I here acknowledge and greatly appreciate their help.

If the sketch is of some interest and if any of the incidents give encouragement to my dear ones I shall be very happy and feel fully repaid for the effort.

Mary Ann Hafen
Bunkerville, Nevada
August, 1938

CONTENTS

ILLUSTRATIONS

CONTENTS

ILLUSTRATIONS

PART I

FROM SWITZERLAND TO UTAH

FROM SWITZERLAND TO UTAH

I was born May 5, 1854, in the valley of Rotenback, about three miles from the city of Bern, Switzerland. I was the second child of my parents, Samuel Stucki and Magdalena Stettler Stucki. My brother John was three years older than I. Our home was surrounded by rolling hills, covered with timber and an undergrowth of moss, shrubbery, and wild berries. Close by we could see the high peaks of the Alps, always white with snow. Our house was a comfortable two-story building braced against a hill, with a stall for the cow near the house and a hayshed above it. Between the stall and the house was my father's workshop. Father was a carpenter, and his shop contained a turning machine with which he fashioned the legs and the carved parts of his furniture.

I remember our large kitchen with its pine floor scrubbed snowy white, and the big stone oven in the corner with its genial warmth. We children used to sit on the little stone bench attached to the oven, and to press our backs against the heavy slabs till we felt their steady

13

warmth creep through and through us. We would go out-of-doors with father when he fed the oven with bundles of twigs from the forest nearby; or watch him sweep out the ashes when mother was to bake her week's supply of bread.

Upstairs were the bedrooms. In cold weather we children used to cuddle between two feather beds. Outside of the house stood a large cherry tree which was very beautiful, especially in spring; and a giant linden tree which was loaded each May with snowy blossoms. I have walked through many orchards since, but those linden flowers of my childhood days seem to be more fragrant than any others I have ever smelled. People said the blossoms might be used for medicine, but so far as I know, their greatest value was the delight they gave us children.

My father owned a small farm consisting of hayland and a little garden. Often in the cool of the morning I followed him thru the dewy grass to the foot of the lot where he mowed the fresh, sweet mountain hay with his long bright scythe. I remember dropping potatoes on the hillside and carrying off rocks from the land. During the summer we children had such fun gathering wild berries in our baskets.

We used to eat them in our bread and milk, and mother often made jam and jelly from them.

Every Sunday mother would dress us in our Sunday clothes to go to church, as we belonged to the Christian Church. One day my Uncle John Reber, who had married my father's sister, came to see us. He was a young man then, about twenty I guess. I remember watching him as he came through the lot, leaning heavily on two crutches, his hands warped and misshapen with rheumatism, and a great hump on his back.

He told us that he had been to a Mormon meeting and that he believed they taught the true gospel of Christ. He told how a short time before, he had had a strange dream. He thought he saw a clear stream of water falling from a clear sky. Then he was impressed that if he could drink from that stream, he would know if their gospel was the true Church of Christ. Just then the stream moved toward him and he drank until he was satisfied. When the Elders (missionaries) came to his home he was convinced that this was the stream he had dreamed of.

Soon after this the Elders called at our home. They talked to my parents for a while and then asked us to join them in prayer. I still remember the sweet influence which I felt during this prayer, though I was only a child. My brother John said he felt the same. He often stated that he even felt blessed when they laid their hats on his bed.

Father's mother had once foretold that men from the far West would come preaching the true gospel of Christ. She said she would not live to see them but that her children would and she wanted them to take them in and receive their teachings. Shortly after her death the first Mormon Elders came to our part of Switzerland.

I well remember the day my Uncle John Reber was baptized. He was the first to join the church in that section. It was mid-winter and the ice over the lake was more than a foot thick. He came down on his crutches to where they had picked through the ice. As he was helped into the water he handed his crutches to a friend who stood near. When he came out he walked on without them, while icicles froze on all his clothes before he could get them changed. Never again in all his life did he use crutches. The hump disappeared entirely, and his hands became straight.

Soon after, my parents also joined the Church and made ready to go to Zion. Father tried to sell our property, but was unable to dispose of it, so he was forced to hire an auctioneer. In this way we received very little for our belongings. Mother took with us a large trunk of clothes, some blankets, a feather bed, and a bolt of linen to make up. Father took only his tool chest. This was early in the year 1860.

Just before we left, my Grandmother Stettler called and tried to persuade us not to go. She was afraid we would be drowned, and could see no reason why we should leave a comfortable home where my father could make a good living, and go far away to a strange land where we did not even know the language.

My father hired a neighbor to take us by horse team and wagon to the city of Bern. Here we stopped one day and night sight-seeing. Since it was my first experience in a city, I well remember looking in at the shop windows and at the beautiful dolls. How I cried for one! But of course I had no money, and besides we had more than we could take already.

I remember also visiting the bear pit. I suppose it was about fifteen feet across. In the center, a large pole with pegs through it gave the bears a chance to climb. My father put me on the rock wall which extended some three feet above the ground and let me look away down into the pit where little cubs were bathing in a pool. Soon one of the big bears came crawling up the pole and I cried to be taken down.

The next day we boarded the train. It took us down along the Rhine River until we crossed a beautiful bridge. Then we boarded a small steam-boat, our first sailing on water. They passed around foamy beer and cake, but the beer was too bitter for me. After sailing some distance we landed in Holland. As we passed through the city of Rotterdam I was delighted with the red brick houses. Never before had I seen a brick dwelling; our mountain cottage was of a finely finished timber, weathered to a grayish brown.

On the shore of the North Sea we boarded a small ship. We went down to a large room under the deck. The floor was covered with a thick layer of straw which came in handy as the sea was very rough. It tossed us about until nearly everyone was sick. I remember mother sitting on the floor with her back against the wall holding the baby and trying to brace herself.

After a day and a night's travel we landed I suppose at Liverpool or thereabouts. As we walked toward the big sail ship awaiting us we were warned by the Elders not to let any stranger carry our bags or children as some had been stolen and sold. I remember how frightened I was when a lady came to my mother and offered to help with her baby. Here we were joined by a large company of emigrants from many countries. There must have been several hundred. As we went on board we were each vaccinated.

When we set sail Uncle John Stucki had to stay behind as he was sick with smallpox. For weeks we were on the Atlantic Ocean. As we children played around, sometimes we stood and watched the cooks kill chickens by wringing their necks. This seemed horrible to me. But after all I remember how good the chicken bones tasted that we picked up after the sailors had thrown them away. I remember with pleasure the evening meetings where we enjoyed the sermons of the Elders and listened to the Mormon hymns which I loved even as a child.

One afternoon while we were playing on the deck one of the sailors pointed out a mermaid. I looked but could see only what seemed to be a lady's head above the water. The sailors told how mermaids would come up to comb their hair and look into a mirror. They said it was a sure sign of storm.

Sure enough there arose a great storm next day. The waves came up like mountains and broke over the deck. We were all ordered under deck and the water splashed on us as we went down the steps. All night the storm raged. Our ship tossed about like a barrel on a wild sea. Two large beams or masts broke off and we were driven many miles back.

We were so frightened that we did not go to bed but stayed in a group about the Elders praying for safety. But though the captain cried out, "We are lost!" we did not give up hope. We had been promised a safe voyage. Next morning the sun came up bright and clear. We all gave thanks to God for our deliverance. The ship was repaired and we had pleasant sailing the rest of the way.

At last we saw the lights of New York City. How the people did shout and toss their hats in the air for joy! I remember best my first meal on shore, because we were served with good light bread and sweet milk. After long weeks of *zweiback,* or hard tack, and dried pea soup, this was a happy change.

In New York we boarded the train with a company from Switzerland, among them Samuel Wittwer and family. On our trip to the Missouri River I remember that Brother Wittwer had an accordion and harmonica to help pass the time.

When we reached Florence, Nebraska, near present Omaha, we were forced to stop for a while because there were not teams enough to take us across the plains to Salt Lake City. The men set to work making handcarts and my father, being a carpenter, helped to make thirty-three of them. Ours was a small two-wheeled vehicle with two shafts and a cover on top. The carts were very much like those the street sweepers use in the cities today, except that ours were made entirely of wood without even an iron rim.

When we came to load up our belongings we found that we had more than we could take. Mother was forced to leave behind her feather bed, the bolt of linen, two large trunks full of clothes, and some other valuable things which we needed so badly later. Father could take only his most necessary tools.

My son Roy in his research in Western history, has made a special study of the hand-cart companies that crossed the Plains to Utah, from 1856 to 1860. There were 2,969 persons, using 662 carts. Five of the companies crossed in 1856. The last two of these started too late —leaving Florence on August 16 and 27 respectively. They were caught by early snows in present Wyoming and suffered terribly. The fourth company, comprising 500 persons, lost over sixty; and the fifth company, of 576 persons, lost between 135 and 150 through freezing and starvation. Compared to them, our company was very fortunate and got along real well.

He says our company was the tenth and last to cross the Plains in handcarts. We had crossed the ocean in the *William Tapscott*, leaving England on May 11th and reaching New York on June 16th. There were 731 Mormons on board this vessel, including 312 from Scandinavia and 85 from Switzerland. Not all of these were to go by handcart, however.

Our company was organized with Oscar O. Stoddard as captain. It contained 126 persons with twenty-two handcarts and three provision wagons drawn by oxen. We set out from Florence on July 6, 1860, for our thousand-mile trip. There were six to our cart. Father and mother pulled it; Rosie (two years old) and Christian (six months old) rode; John (nine) and I (six) walked. Sometimes, when it was down hill, they let me ride too.

The first night out the mosquitoes gave us a hearty welcome. Father had bought a cow to take along, so we could have milk on the way. At first he tied her to the back of the cart, but she would sometimes hang back, so he thought he would make a harness and have her pull the cart while he led her. By this time mother's feet were so swollen that she could not wear shoes, but had to wrap her feet with cloth. Father thought that by having the cow pull the cart mother might ride. This worked well for some time.

One day a group of Indians came riding up on horses. Their jingling trinkets, dragging poles and strange appearance frightened the cow and sent her chasing off with the cart and children. We were afraid that the children might be killed, but the cow fell into a deep gully and the cart turned upside down. Although the children were under the trunk and bedding, they were unhurt, but after that father did not hitch the cow to the cart again. He let three Danish boys take her to hitch to their cart. Then the Danish boys, each in turn, would help father pull our cart.

Of course we had many other difficulties. One was that it was hard for the carts to keep up with the three provision wagons drawn by ox teams. Often the men pulling the carts would try to take shortcuts through the brush and sand in order to keep up.

After about three weeks my mother's feet became better so she could wear her shoes again. She would get so discouraged and down-hearted; but father never lost courage. He would always cheer her up by telling her that we were going to Zion, that the Lord would take care of us, and that better times were coming.

Even when it rained the company did not stop traveling. A cover on the handcart shielded the two younger children. The rest of us found it more comfortable moving than standing still in the drizzle. In fording streams the men often carried the children and weaker women across on their backs. The company stopped over on Sundays for rest, and meetings were held for spiritual comfort and guidance. At night, when the handcarts were drawn up in a circle and the fires were lighted, the camp looked quite happy. Singing, music and speeches by the leaders cheered everyone. I remember that we stopped one night at an old Indian camp ground. There were many bright-colored beads in the ant hills.

At times we met or were passed by the overland stage coach with its passengers and mail bags and drawn by four fine horses. When the Pony Express dashed past it seemed almost like the wind racing over the prairie.

Our provisions began to get low. One day a herd of buffalo ran past and the men of our company shot two of them. Such a feast as we had when they were dressed. Each family was given a piece of meat to take along. My brother John, who pushed at the back of our cart, used to tell how hungry he was all the time and how tired he got from pushing. He said he felt that if he could just sit down for a few minutes he would feel so much better. But instead, father would ask if he couldn't push a little harder. Mother was nursing the baby and could not help much, especially when the food ran short and she grew weak. When rations were reduced father gave mother a part of his share of the food, so he was not so strong either.

When we got that chunk of buffalo meat father put it in the handcart. My brother John remembered that it was the fore part of the week and that father said we would save it for Sunday dinner. John said, "I was so very hungry and the meat smelled so good to me while pushing at the handcart that I could not resist. I had a little pocket knife and with it

I cut off a piece or two each half day. Although I expected a severe whipping when father found it out, I cut off little pieces each day. I would chew them so long that they got white and perfectly tasteless. When father came to get the meat he asked me if I had been cutting off some of it. I said 'Yes, I was so hungry I could not let it alone.' Instead of giving me a scolding or whipping, father turned away and wiped tears from his eyes."

Even when we were on short rations, if we met a band of Indians the Captain of our Company would give them some of the provisions so the Indians would let us go by in safety. Food finally became so low that word was sent to Salt Lake City and in about two weeks fresh supplies arrived.

At last, when we reached the top of Emigration Canyon, overlooking Salt Lake, on that September day, 1860, the whole company stopped to look down through the valley. Some yelled and tossed their hats in the air. A shout of joy arose at the thought that our long trip was over, that we had at last reached Zion, the place of rest. We all gave thanks to God for helping us safely over the Plains and mountains to our destination.

When we arrived in the city we were welcomed by the people who came out carrying baskets of fruit and other kinds of good things to eat. Even though we could not understand their language, they made us feel that we were among friends.

We were invited home by a good family who kept us two or three days, until my parents were rested. Then we were given a little house near the river Jordan, three miles from town, and father was put to work on the public road. He was paid in produce, mostly flour and potatoes, from the Tithing Office.

We stayed here all that winter and though we were poor we did not suffer for food and shelter. While we lived here my brother and I used to go fishing. One Sunday the bank on which John was standing caved off and he fell in. The river was deep and he could not swim. I ran and called Mother. She brought a long pole for him to hold to but he could not hear her call. He was washed down stream until he came to a bridge. He happened to catch hold of one of the posts supporting the bridge and was able to climb out. As soon as he was safe he fainted and Mother had a hard time bringing him to.

Part II

PIONEER LIFE IN SOUTHERN UTAH

PIONEER LIFE IN SOUTHERN UTAH

In the fall of 1861 father and his family were called to go with the Swiss Company to settle southern Utah — a Dixieland where grapes and cotton could be raised. Since many of the Swiss people had cultivated grapes in the old country, they were selected for this special mission. Many of the emigrants, like ourselves, had no teams of their own, so the Church provided transportation. Teams were relayed at various stations along the way. One man hauled us from Salt Lake to Provo, another on to Payson, and still another on to the next town; and so on until we arrived at Fort Clara on the Santa Clara Creek, late in November.

Until father could rig up some sort of shelter we were taken into the school house. The little town, previously established as an Indian mission, housed about twenty families. Also there was a grist mill, and a rock fort about a hundred feet square, with walls about twelve feet high and two feet thick. Many of the emigrants were given temporary shelter in the rooms inside the fort, while a new town was being laid out. The old town, situated around the point of the hill from where Santa Clara now stands, was thought to be too near the creek and consequently in danger of being flooded.

On the "lower flat," about a mile from the old settlement, the new townsite was platted. Daniel Bonelli, who could speak both German and English, was put in charge. Distribution of the lots was made by drawing for numbers. When the lots were assigned, they were dedicated by prayer and song. Everyone went immediately to work and soon all sorts of shelters sprang up among the dry, dead sunflowers and the gray rabbitbrush.

Many of those who had covered wagons used their wagon boxes for their first shelters. We had none, so father built a sort of wigwam out of willows. To mother this seemed a poor substitute for the nice house left behind.

"Oh, these red hills! this roily water!" she would sometimes say as she remembered the green hills and clear mountain streams of Switzerland.

But when the lots were plowed up and set to vineyards, a dam built across the creek, and irrigation ditches dug, things looked more promising.

Real trouble began, however, when persistent rain set in. For days and days it did not let up. Winter winds chilled us through and through as we huddled together in our leaky shanty.

My Uncle John Stucki had built a shelter of posts and willows which he plastered inside and out with mud, and covered with a good dirt roof. He invited us to stay with him until the rain stopped. We were very crowded but we could at least keep dry.

The rain continued falling; and the creek, which had been so narrow in places that we could step across it, now swelled till it spread from bluff to bluff and became a terrible, muddy river. Sometimes great masses of driftwood obstructed the channel and almost threw the raging waters into other courses.

The little farms and cottonwood trees that grew in the bottom lands were being swept away. And everybody feared for the old town.

One night when we were sleeping, the creek rose higher and higher. Its thick roaring waters laden with brush and trees torn from the ground along its course swept all before it. Not only the old town, but the sturdy rock fort, thought to be out of the reach of the flood, was washed away. Jacob Hamblin's valuable grist mill, too, was lost. This was in January, 1862. On the "lower flat" we were untouched by the flood.

When the water went down, dams and ditches had to be rebuilt. With a borrowed shovel father spaded a garden plot on our lot and planted seeds which mother had carefully carried from the old country. While waiting for vegetables to grow we used "pig weeds" for greens. This weed is a kind of wild spinach. That, with a small portion of bread was our menu day in and day out.

Father's next interest was to provide us a better shelter. The dugout he built was about six feet deep, twelve feet square, with a slanting roof. Crevices between the roof poles were filled with small compact bundles of rushes held in place by a weaving of young willows. About a six-inch layer of dirt which had been excavated from the cellar was then put on the roof. There were no windows. The front and only door had one small pane of glass to light up the cool cozy room within.

Beds were made by driving corner posts into the dirt floor. Black willow poles split were nailed close together to serve as slats on the bed and fresh straw was used for mattresses. Comfortable pillows were made from the fluff of the cat-tails which were gathered from the sloughs along the creek. To save space in

this little room-of-all-purposes, an improvised
table was made by laying a large plank on top
of the posts of one of the beds. Two benches
made of boards, a shelf cupboard, and a small
sheet-iron stove with two holes and a tiny oven,
completed the furnishings. All in all the little
primitive shelter was quite comfortable; for it
was pleasantly cool in the suffocating heat of
the summer, and was warm in the winter months
when light snow fell, rain drizzled, or ice coated
the water ditches. For three years this dug-out
was to serve as our home.

To cultivate his lands, father hired a team
and plow from an old settler, and paid for the
use with labor. That first year he planted
grain. But during July and August nearly
everything dried up. He got only eight bushels
from his hard labor. But he paid his tithing
out of that saying, "The Lord will bless the
nine parts left to last longer."

Most of that summer we had to carry our
water from a spring about a mile and a half
away. Some of the settlers even carried water
by the bucketful to keep their young trees from
dying.

That fall we were facing a winter with
no food, so father set out on foot to Cedar City
to find work. He started without food, leav-

ing what little there was, for his family. When he was about half way to Cedar, fifty miles or so from home, he met Casper Gubler, one of our neighbors, driving home from a trip to the north. Father was so dizzy from hunger that he could scarcely walk straight. When Casper saw him reeling along the road he called out and asked if he was drunk. Father replied, "Only hungry. I've had nothing to eat for three days." At that, Casper fed him with bread and meat to strengthen father for his further journey.

He made his way to Cedar City where he got work as a carpenter and received pay in provisions, wheat and potatoes. To haul his stuff home he had to go clear back to Santa Clara to get a team and wagon. By this time it was late in the fall, and cold weather was setting in. On his final journey home with the provisions the potatoes froze, and as he drove into town, water was running from the bottom of the wagon box out of the thawing potatoes. We had to eat them, though. I remember that they tasted good—pleasantly sweet—but we children would cry with the stomach-ache after each meal.

The next spring father worked and got more land on which he raised a good crop in

MR. AND MRS. SAMUEL STUCKI AND FAMILY (About 1885)
Standing: Mary Ann, John S. (photograph taken while on mission to Switzerland and inserted here), Rosena.
Sitting: Samuel, Magdalena S., Christian.

spite of the scarcity of water. Many of the settlers had become discouraged and moved away. President Brigham Young, visiting us, told the settlers to be of good cheer, that they should live to see the day when there would be water enough to take out on the benchlands. Some people did not believe this but it has come to pass.

The second summer we were in Santa Clara mother took three of us children with her up to the Three-Mile Place, three miles above town, to glean wheat. We gleaned, threshed with a flail, and cleaned four two-bushel sacks full of clean wheat in one week while we camped there. We gleaned in the fields for several years.

The men decided to build a better canal to bring more water to town. As they were digging around the point of the hill a big bank caved down on the workers and my father was entirely covered up. I remember how they came carrying him home on a sheet, six men. His back was injured and his body was all bruised and it seemed impossible for him to live, but through the blessing of God and the adminis-tration of the Elders he was gradually healed and able again to provide for his family.

As time passed the dugouts and willow

shanties of the town were replaced by adobe houses. Whenever I had time I liked to watch the men make the adobes. Sand from the river bed, and clay from the ground surface on their own lots, were mixed with water and stirred with a shovel until smooth. This was then poured into molds that had been sanded; then turned onto the ground to bake in the hot sun. Each mold held three adobes. Every day the adobes were turned until they were thoroughly dry.

With the help of the neighbors, father built us an adobe house. A hole about four feet deep was dug. Rocks were quarried in the hills nearby. With sand-and-clay mortar they were laid up in a rock foundation. With this same smooth plaster the adobe walls were laid up—two adobes deep, making a substantial wall a foot thick. Instead of the sand roofs of the old houses, wooden rafters covered with sheeting and shingles hauled in from the North made a water-tight shelter. In each room was a window or two with panes of glass.

By this time, along each side of the wide street ran a little irrigating ditch of water. Upon the banks, to shade the sidewalks, cotton-wood trees were set out. Every morning while the water was still cool and clean, each family dipped up barrels of water for household and drinking purposes. After a storm the water was roily and had to settle before it was fit to use.

Water for laundry purposes was generally softened by pouring in cottonwood ashes. Soft rainwater we generally used to wash our hair and our nicest clothes. But of course we couldn't get rain water always. A favorite substitute for soap was the root of the "oose," or yucca, sometimes called "soap root." This root looked about like a sugarbeet. Cut up and left in water it soon made a fluffy suds. Colored clothes came out fresh and bright because the cleanser did not harm the dyes. White clothes however were turned slightly yellow by it and therefore were not generally washed with oose. I remember how soft, fluffy, and sweet-smelling my hair always felt after a shampoo with oose suds. For mopping the wooden floors the oose root served not only as soap but as scrubbing brush as well. And how white and beautiful those floors would look.

While hay was still scarce, we hoed up the secarta growing like a carpet upon the sandy foothills, and carried it home by the sackfull to feed the cows during milking time. By day the cows were herded upon the bench or upon the hills nearby. The hardest time of my life were the years when my brother John and I had to take the town herd of milk cows on the Clara bench to feed and watch all day long. We would go up near the red mountain where the town of Ivins now is, carrying with us a quart can of water and a small lunch. During the summer the sand would become so hot our bare feet would nearly blister and we would run from bush to bush for shade. Then every noon we would have to take the cows to water at the three mile place, back to the bench for the after- noon, and home at night. Many times we would nearly choke for want of water. Sometimes John would have to lead me home, as I would be so weary and thirsty that I had to lie down, saying I could not go home because I was too tired.

One day as John and I were sitting under a bush watching the cows there came a large animal around the herd, heading toward where we were sitting. As I remember it now it seemed to have a large bushy head. It must have been a mountain lion. There were four or five horses grazing around us. When they saw this animal they ran toward it, attacking it with their feet and biting it. They drove it rapidly down to- ward the creek until all we could see was a

cloud of dust.   To me this always seemed to be
a case of divine protection.

Another disagreeable task that I had to do
in those days was to walk to St. George, five
miles in the hot sun, and ask for the watering
turn.   Once I remember meeting an Indian who
frightened me.

In those early years, most of the people in
Santa Clara were Swiss.   They continued to
speak the German language.   But the children, mixing with the English, soon learned
to speak English.   And finally most of the
grown people learned English too.   Preaching
at the church meetings was sometimes in German and sometimes in English.   Our family
prayers were always in German until after we
moved to Bunkerville.

The first school I attended was the winter
I was ten years old.   I had no shoes; in fact,
I never had shoes until I was nearly a grown
woman.   But this year there was a heavy snow.
As I went to school my hands and arms began
to itch and the hives broke out in blisters.   I
asked my teacher if I might go home and, when
he saw my red hands and arms, he said I
might.   But the trip back through the snow
barefooted caused the hives to go in on me.
I was taken with a burning fever and a pain in

my stomach. For three weeks I was very sick.

As I had no bed except a pile of straw covered with old clothes my back became raw and sore. At last Sister Graff took pity on me and loaned me a feather pillow to lie on. I think nothing has ever seemed so comfortable to me since. But that was a habit in those early days—for neighbors to be kindly. And those earliest settlers, how kind they were to us Swiss emigrants. I shall always remember Jacob Hamblin; his good honest face; his pleasant voice; his tall, slender frame. Whenever he spoke in church his words filled us all with joy and satisfaction. And Dudley Leavitt was so good to us too. He frequently brought flour to distribute to the different families and also meat when he killed a beef.

During those earliest years our Sabbath services were held under a big cottonwood tree. Then the people built a meeting house where we could have dances and socials as well as church and school. For our dance orchestra we had a violin, an accordion, and a horn.

As soon as the settlers had enough ahead to buy trees and shrubs, they drove all the way to California to buy young fruit trees and grapevine cuttings. In our mild warm climate of southern Utah we soon had peaches, apples and luscious grapes to vary the diet.

By this time cotton was rather common. One of President Young's objects in sending the people to settle southern Utah had been that they might raise cotton there. Cotton seed was brought to Santa Clara and planted. Then a cotton gin was brought in. My father and his brother built the gin house and the water-wheel to furnish the power to run the gin. Once, after the gin was running, father caught his hand in it and the teeth tore his hand quite badly.

We had not yet planted cotton for ourselves. But we children were permitted to glean those partly opened bolls that were left after the neighbors had done with their fields. We gathered several sackfulls. By the firelight in the evenings we shelled out the cotton. We dried it further in the sun. And then I traded mine to a peddler for calico. How well I remember that first new dress. I thought it very beautiful. It was yellow with little red and blue flowers. As we had no sewing machine, I made the dress by hand with my aunt's help. I was then twelve years old. In the six years that I had been in America I had never had an honest-to-goodness new dress. Everything I wore was made from mother's old dresses. So this new calico dress made me feel like a queen.

This very same year I learned how to weave. Father made me a loom. My arms were too short to reach both sides of the loom to shove my shuttle through the web, so I had to lean from side to side. I was proud of the first dress I wove. It was made in a checkered pattern one inch across of brown, blue, and white, from cotton yarn. I also made what we called jeans out of cotton warp with wool. This was used for men's suits and was very heavy cloth.

Before this, father made me a spinning wheel. I was so glad that father was a carpenter; he could make us so many nice things that others did not have. After we had gathered the cotton, picked out the seeds and carded it, I spun it into threads on my wheel. We dyed our yarn different colors. We used evergreen brush for dye. Also we used dock roots for brown, adding a little coperas for dark brown. We made blue with indigo; red from the red berries which grew along the creek.

When the cotton factory was built at

Washington, ten miles away, we could take our raw cotton and exchange it for cloth, or for yarn if we wished to weave our own.

Besides making our dresses we also made our hats. We cut the ripe wheat straws, using only the long top joint. We would lay a handful of this straw in the water until it became soft. Then we braided it. I became expert at braiding from seven to thirteen straws. When the strip of braid was about eight yards long we sewed it around and around, shaping it into a hat. I shaped the crown over a little bucket and pressed the top, sides and rim with a hot flatiron. Our Sunday hats we made of split bleached straw. For bleaching purposes, we removed the head of a barrel; tacked the hats inside; lighted a plate of sulphur; covered the barrel tight so the smoke could not escape; and the hats came out bleached a pure white. We decorated our hats with ornaments made of straw dyed different colors.

I guess through those years I made enough hats to fill a wagon box. I would trade them to the neighbors for things which we needed. I remember making a nice hat for Brother Holt. It was white and turned up around the edge. In exchange for it he made me a potato masher and rolling pin out of nice white cottonwood. I have them yet.

When I was a girl I helped father harvest a lot of grain. We cut it with a sickle and bound it by hand. In addition to our own grain, we cut for others on shares, receiving four bushels to the acre. Father, John, Rosie and I would cut an acre in a day, by working early and late. My, how our backs would ache and how the sweat would roll off us. One year, I remember, I helped father sickle nine acres. That was the last year before I was married.

When I was fourteen, Mother had a baby girl. It was the first baby in our family for so long that we all loved her. But when she was a year and a half old she died with black canker. Two years later a fine baby brother was born but he also died, with chills and fever. We did not know much about medicine because, in the old country, we had always relied upon a doctor. Gradually we learned home remedies after much sad experience.

For amusements, as young people, we had dances, candy pullings, shucking bees, and horseback and wagon rides. On May Day and other special occasions, we would go up to the

Three Mile Place and put up big swings under the large cottonwood trees and have fine lunches and all kinds of sports. We occasionally went swimming, girls and boys separately, of course, and sometimes we caught fish in the creek.

At the dances we danced the quadrille, hoursles four, minuet, waltz and schottische. The music was the violin or the accordion at first. Then a brass band was organized and it played for the dances and for celebrations.

The church meetings were social occasions too. There was both a Swiss and an English choir. I belonged to the Swiss, with George Staheli as chorister. We would have choir practice once a week.

As a young woman I took an interest in parties, dances and different kinds of fun. Naturally, I had young men callers. But none of them appealed to me so much as did John Reber, my uncle who had been so miraculously healed in the Old Country. He was much older than I, was married to my father's sister, and had four children. But he was kind and jolly and everybody liked him.

At this time the law of Plural Marriage was being practiced in the Church, and the authorities recommended that the men who were able to provide for more than one family should marry again. In this way more persons in the spirit world would have the opportunity to come to this earth and have bodies. It would also build up the Church and the country faster. Many did not want to go into polygamy, but felt that it was their religious duty to do so when advised by the Church authorities.

John Hafen called and took me to several dances. John Reber did not dance, so I had not been out much with him, but when he asked me to marry him I was ready to say yes. His wife, Aunt Barbara, helped me make my wedding outfit, a simple dress of blue material with little pink flowers and a white petticoat. I was then nineteen years old.

My sister Rosie was to be married too. So we decided to make it a double wedding. We had to go all the way to Salt Lake City to be married in the Endowment House, for the temple in St. George or the one in Salt Lake had not been built yet. With our two outfits loaded with dried peaches for the northern brewery, we set out that July morning, 1873. Rosie's husband-to-be was a widower and his mother traveled along with us. Our ten days of travel to Salt Lake were happy ones. It was interesting to see so much country and the northern towns. We were married on August 4th. In ten days more we were back again in Santa Clara, happy and satisfied with our lot.

The day after we returned home, my husband took me and Aunt Barbara and her four children for a ride down to the field to see how the crops looked. We started back feeling very happy that the corn was so thrifty. On the way one of the horses caught its bridle under the wagon tongue, pulled off the bridle, and started running. I jumped off; so did Aunt Barbara and the children. The frightened horses turned down a lane, ran over a woodpile, threw my husband under the wagon, where two wheels ran over him. He was injured internally and in spite of all we could do for him he died the next day.

This was a sad finish to my honeymoon, and I went back home to live with mother and father. Inasmuch as they were getting old and times were hard, they thought it best that I should marry again.

Soon John Hafen came courting me. He had been born in Schurzingen, Canton Thurgau, Switzerland, on October 17, 1838, and emigrated to America with his father and sister Barbara in 1861. His father had saved up some money in Switzerland and before setting out for the trip across the Plains from Florence, Nebraska, bought four wagons, fourteen yoke of oxen and two milch cows. John rode a mule across the Plains and drove the milch cows and other loose cattle. They traveled in the Sextus E. Johnston company and arrived safely in Salt Lake City in September, 1861.

In a few weeks they were called as part of the Swiss Company to settle in southern Utah. They were in the same company as my parents in the move to Santa Clara. John had married Susette Bosshard in Salt Lake City in October, 1861, just before the Swiss company set out for southern Utah.

When John asked me to marry him, I hesitated at first. But my parents urged me to consent, saying what a fine man he was and that by waiting I would probably do worse. Susette was opposed to his marrying again, but the authorities advised him to do so anyway, saying that she would be reconciled. I did not like to marry him under those circumstances, but being urged on by him and my parents, I consented.

So just three months after my first trip north, I was journeying again to Salt Lake City. Again the wagon was loaded with dried peaches

JOHN GEORGE HAFEN
At ages twenty-one and forty-five

for the brewery. Christian Wittwer and Sister Frehner (a widow) were going along too, to be married in Salt Lake. On the way up, Sister Frehner cut out and made me a dress. She offered to make it, as she knew I had but one to travel in. This trip seemed different from the first one. I cried when I left home, and cried often all the way up and back. John was kind to me and did everything he could to comfort and please me, but somehow I was not happy. We were married on November 24th, in the Endowment House.

When we got back to Santa Clara we set up housekeeping in a two-room adobe house that had belonged to his father, who had died ten years before. John would stay at my place one day and at Susette's the next and we got along pretty well at first. But Susette seemed unable to reconcile herself to my coming into the family. Gradually he began to neglect me.

Finally, I told him that if he could not treat us alike I would leave him. But I doubted whether it was right to do so. So I fasted and prayed to find out what would be right to do. After three days of fasting I woke in the night. The indifference and bitterness had gone from my heart and I loved him and forgave him for his neglect. I could hardly wait until morning to tell John my change of feeling. In the morning, after I had my work done, I went up town and found him talking to some neighbors. I told him what had happened and said I would stay with him if he would treat me right. He promised to do so, and after that, for several years we lived happy.

At the time that my first baby, Albert, was born—September 4, 1874—I nearly lost my life with a hemorrhage. Sister Listen attended me. But I got up out of bed on the tenth day, for that was the prescribed time when a woman should resume her household duties after childbirth. For three months the baby cried with colic. Often I rocked his cradle with my foot while I did my washing, sewing and cooking. One night he cried so much that my husband took him away and gave him a whisky sling. He slept soundly the rest of the night.

I had a little experience in regard to the Word of Wisdom. Before I was married we never used tea, coffee, or tobacco, and very seldom a little diluted wine. But when I was married, John wanted tea for breakfast and so I took to drinking it with him for about three months. By that time I became so nervous and trembling that I couldn't hold my needle steady enough to sew a decent stitch, and at that time I didn't have a sewing machine. I thought it was my drinking tea that made me nervous, so I stopped it. In a few months I got over the nervousness. So I know that the Word of Wisdom was given for our good.

Early in 1874, while President Brigham Young was in St. George, he had told the people he wanted them to join together and live the United Order, or the Order of Enoch. Orders were organized in St. George and in other towns. One was formed in Santa Clara. Everyone was to share according to his or her needs and the crops were to be raised, harvested and shared in common. My husband was appointed to market the community produce, as he was especially successful in peddling fruit at the mining camps and the northern towns. But the plan did not work very well. People were too jealous and selfish and did not act according to the will of the Lord. The Order soon broke up and the families went back to the old way of living.

Father and a few others thought that they should try it again; that perhaps they had not been humble and prayerful enough to live this holy Order. So father with his second wife, Christian Wittwer and family, and a few others went to join the Order at Price, on the Virgin River, a little below St. George. As mother stayed with her family in Santa Clara, I went to Price with father to stay a week or so on a visit. I certainly enjoyed the friendly spirit that prevailed there. Each woman seemed to be willing and ready to do her share in cooking, sewing and housework. Everyone ate at one table in a large room. Each man did his share in the work that had to be done. How nice it would have been if they could have continued in that fine spirit. But jealousies and difficulties arose and the United Order broke up there just as it had done in Santa Clara.

Bishop Edward Bunker of Santa Clara wanted to give the Order another trial, so he got Dudley Leavitt and others to join him and they went down the Virgin River into Nevada and started the town of Bunkerville. The Order worked successfully for three years, until the town was well under way. Then it disbanded.

President Brigham Young tried to get the silk industry started in southern Utah. We took some part in the move. The Relief Society ladies took turns feeding the silk worms with mulberry leaves in the upper room of the Relief Society House in Santa Clara. When I would

take my turn it would almost make me crawl
to see the little, wiggly, white worms crawl
about over the leaves. When the worms were
full grown they were from two to two and one-
half inches long and a little more slender than
a tomato worm. If I remember right, it took
about three weeks feeding before the worms
would wrap themselves up in a cocoon of fine
silk. The weaver had to unwrap and spin several threads together to make the weaving yarn
the right thickness. Some cloth was made in
St. George but the industry did not prove very
successful.

When my little boy, Albert, was two years
old John was called on a six month's mission to
the German-speaking people of Minnesota. One
night while I was alone Albert took very sick
with a burning fever. I thought I was going to
lose him. For a whole week the fever raged.
Finally, through fasting and prayer, he re-
covered. Later he was troubled with queer
spells. He would cry out in his sleep and jump
up in his bed. I was worried, so had Brother
Tyler give him a patriarchal blessing. In that
he was promised health, that he should grow
to maturity and go on a mission. After that
I did not worry about him.

Shortly after my husband returned from his

mission we moved into a little one-room, sod-roofed house below town. This was just before Mary, my second child, was born. I was troubled with chills and fever and finally a painful felon developed. I poulticed my finger with gravy and with bread and milk but it kept getting worse. Finally, after I had lost my sleep for about a week because of pain, my father came and administered to me. Shortly after, with my hand on my chest, I fell asleep and did not wake until the sun was high in the sky next day. A few hours later the felon broke and continued to heal from then on.

When Mary came, November 5, 1877, Sister Frehner attended me. As usual I got up on the tenth day. I suppose I caught cold from the draughts that came up through the loose boards in the floor. At any rate I had to go back to bed for three weeks and came very near dying. My sister Rosie brought her young baby with her and did up my work each day. I drank barley gruel morning, noon, and night and it helped me. When my young baby was just six weeks old she took chills and fever. She was very sick and fainted away several times. After she got over this, however, she was the best baby I ever had. Often when I went to pick cotton I took her to the fields. There she would lie contentedly all day sucking her thumb, except for the moments when I took her up to feed her.   My little boy Albert would play about while I worked.

At the birth of my third child, Bertha, November 24, 1881, I was troubled with sinking spells, nearly suffocating at times. Sister Frehner attended me again. My sister Rosie came and did up my work each day, and my husband took care of me at night.   About six months after this John moved me into a better house. He had bought Bishop Edward Bunker's place, after the Bishop went down to start Bunkerville.

Shortly afterward John was called to go on a mission to Switzerland.   Before he left he told Johnnie, Susette's oldest son, to see that I was always supplied with wood, and to help me in every way he could.   And Johnnie did it.   My husband left in the spring of 1882 and returned in 1884. The brass band and most of the people of the town went out to welcome him. The band always went out to meet returning missionaries.

During the two years that he was away, I dried enough peaches on shares to buy me a sewing machine.   My father and I would go to his orchard at day-break while the children were still sleeping and get a wagon load of peaches. Then I would cut them and put them on board scaffolds to dry in the sun. I got half of all I dried. Peddlers took the dried fruit to Salt Lake City and brought back cash for it. In this way I raised most of the forty-two dollars for the machine. It was a White. I bought it from Woolley, Lund and Judd of St. George. I still have the machine and it runs well to this day, though the top box cover was broken years ago.

With my new machine I sewed for other people to help support my family while John was away. I could not help him out much, though once I sold a calf for five dollars and sent the money to him.

John had no sooner returned from his mission in 1884 than he was called to be Bishop of the Santa Clara Ward, a position he held for the next twenty-eight years. He took the place of Marius Ensign, who had died. Later in this year he married a young emigrant girl whom he had known while on his mission to Switzerland —Anna Huber. He sent her to live with me. Here she stayed for two years. In February, 1885, he married my sister Rosie, who was then a widow with two children.

In the 1880's, when the Government sent marshals to arrest polygamists, John tried to keep out of their way. But he met them two or three times in a kindly way, treating them with wine, and they told afterwards that they wouldn't arrest a man who was taking care of the widows. The United States marshals that came to Santa Clara were Armstrong and Mc-Geary. We hated the sound of their names.

Several times when I heard that marshals were in town, I took my children and some sewing, went across the creek into the field and stayed there until night. Then John moved Anna and me over to St. George, where we stayed for two months, when the marshals were most active. John was never arrested.

On the twelfth of March, 1885, Selena was born. Sister Keller, a neighbor who lived across the street, attended me and came each day to wash the baby; and Anna looked after the housework while I was sick. I got through with this birth pretty well and also with the next two children. This baby, Selena, was a very restless child.

A child was born to Anna in August, so they called him August. He was a fine, husky boy. One morning when he was eight months old we awoke to find the little fellow was dead.

He must have smothered in the bed clothes. It was an awful blow to the young mother, but I comforted her the best I could. The next year Anna was given a house to herself.

In 1887 my son Wilford was born—August 12. When he was about two months old I dreamed that I went to a big celebration at the public square in Santa Clara. Some women were preparing picnic under the trees. I looked up and saw a large, beautiful bird flying around. All at once it came down to where I stood with my baby in my arms. Then it seemed to be a young woman dressed in white. She reached out her arms for my baby, but I said I could not let it go. Then she snatched it from me and flew away. I had no power to hold it. When I awoke I feared that I would not have him long, and I prayed the Lord to lengthen out his stay with us. And He did.

In 1888 John moved Anna down to Littlefield, Arizona. The next year he moved her on to Bunkerville, Nevada.

On July 14, 1890, Lovena, my sixth child, was born in Santa Clara.

MARY ANN HAFEN AND FAMILY (in 1895)
Left to right: Bertha, Wilford, Albert, LeRoy R., Mary Ann, Lovena, Mary, Selena.

PART III

A NEW HOME IN NEVADA

A NEW HOME IN NEVADA

Because Santa Clara had so little land for so many settlers, we decided it would be best for me to take my young family and move to Bunkerville, where a settlement had been started and where there was more and cheaper land. My son Albert was already down there helping John's other wife, Anna.

My birthday occurred the day before we were to leave. Our relatives and friends gathered to give a combined birthday and farewell party.

On May 6, 1891, with me and our five children tucked into a covered wagon, John clucked at the horses and drove away from our old home town. Another wagon, driven by young Johnnie, conveyed our household effects. As neighbors, relatives, and friends crowded about to see us off, I with others shed a few tears. I knew I was going to something of the same hardships I had known in childhood days; that my children were to grow up in a strange land with scarcely a relative near; and that they too would have to share in the hardships of subduing a new country.

Our drive was not unpleasant, however. The country was all new to me as I had never been beyond Santa Clara westward. Past Conger Farm, up Conger Hill, and on to Camp Springs Flat we traveled and there camped for the night. The next day we drove past the Cliffs, and down the long Slope where great Joshua trees looked like soldiers with their helmets and spears. The second night we spent at the Beaver Dams on a clear little creek where gnawed young cottonwoods gave evidence of beaver being present. The next day we passed the beginnings of Littlefield. Then we followed the Virgin River bed, crossed Mesquite flat, where a few farms and shanties showed settlement, again crossed the river, and arrived at Bunkerville.

The little town was rather inviting. In the early dusk the numerous young cottonwoods along the field canals and along the town ditches looked like an oasis in a desert. There was only one fence in the whole town and that was around Samuel Wittwer's lot.

Albert was overjoyed to see us. John's other wife, Anna, had supper waiting for us when we arrived. Among other things she

THE HAFEN HOME AT BUNKERVILLE, NEVADA

Taken in 1917, with Mary Ann Hafen and Ann Woodbury Hafen in the foreground.

served alfalfa greens dressed with white sauce. It was quite a tasty dish.

The next morning we went up to the little place that John had purchased from a Danishman, Brother Jorgensen. It was a two-roomed adobe house with dirt floors and dirt roof. That did not look so inviting, but John promised that he would see that it was soon finished off with a good roof and floors, and probably would put a second story on the house to make more bedrooms.

The big lot already had five or six almond trees growing, and a nice vineyard of grapes. But there was a little wash running through the side of the lot which had to be filled in; and there was only a makeshift fence of mesquite brush piled about three feet high. Besides, the lot was covered with rocks, because it was close to the gravel hill. Our twenty-five-acre farm, about a mile and a half above town, was only partly cleared of arrow weeds and mesquite. It was sandy land with some large sand knolls to be leveled.

The cow we had brought down was dry so John turned her in as part payment on the land. Later another was brought down from Santa Clara. Because of his duties as Bishop in Santa Clara my husband had to hurry back and left

Albert, our sixteen-year-old son, in charge of the planting.

As soon as we could we planted corn, cane, cotton, squashes and melons in the field; and vegetables in the town lot. The brush fences were but poor protection from the stray animals that went foraging about. However we got a pretty good crop from everything planted that year. Albert dug up three young mulberry trees from Mesquite and planted them around our shadeless house. Now, after forty-seven years of growth, those mulberry trees completely shade the old place.

I remember how in those earliest years we were disturbed by the hot winds that swept over the dry bench lands from the south.

That first fall John came back bringing a load of lumber to finish off the house. During the winter he and Albert put in the floors and ceiling; built up the adobe walls to make a second story; and put on a shingle roof. There was no stairway up so the children used a ladder out of doors.

From the first we found that the river dam was far more unstable here than at Santa Clara. Each flood that came down the river broke our Bunkerville dam. Nothing but a loose brush and rock dam seemed feasible here because of

the soft sandy river bottom, which was quite
in contrast to the rocky bottom of the Santa
Clara Creek. Because of this softness, teams
were often stuck in the quicksand and had to
be dug out. Range animals occasionally mired
fast and starved to death in the sandy bars of
the river.

Before we had been in our new location
eight months I became homesick to see the folks
in Santa Clara. So when John took a load of
grain up to the grist mill in Washington, I
went along. It was pretty hard pulling for
his little span of mules so I walked most of
the way up the fifteen-mile Slope above Littlefield, to lighten the load. When at last we
neared the town, at sight of the old familiar
creek, I broke down and cried. And yet from
choice I would not have given up my new home,
poor though it was.

After that, about every year I managed
to make the trip up to see my relatives. And
for a while John came down every month or
so to help Albert and to make small improve-
ments around the place. But being Bishop at
Santa Clara, and with his other three families,
he could not be with us much. So I had to
care for my seven children mostly by myself.
He had provided us a house, lot, and land and

he furnished some supplies. But it was a new country and we had a hard time to make a go of it.

Though we almost always had grain on hand, we sometimes found ourselves without flour. At such times we had to grind the wheat in a coffee mill until we could take a grist to the mill at Washington, sixty-five miles away. We also ground corn in the coffee mill and made mush of it. With molasses and milk on the mush it made our breakfasts for years.

We hauled our loads of cotton to the cotton factory at Washington and received cloth in exchange. I think we got about twelve and one-half cents per pound for cotton in the seed, and paid fifty to sixty cents a yard for jeans —a cotton and woolen mixed cloth.

Sugar, or sorghum, cane we took to the town sorghum mill and got our year's supply of molasses. Sugar and honey were almost unknown in those times, so sorghum served as sweetening. Candy pulls around the shining molasses mill were favorite evening pastimes for the young people. Most every year we made a practice of putting up twenty-gallon barrels of preserves—peaches or green tomatoes. The peaches were washed, dumped whole and unpeeled into the big vats of sorghum. After

cooking to a preserves they were put into barrels.   Green tomatoes were generally gathered
just before frost, soaked over night in salt
water, and then cooked over the furnace fire
with sorghum as sweetener.

After we had been in Bunkerville about
two years, my last child was born—December
8, 1893. He was a fine husky boy, weighing
$12\frac{1}{2}$ pounds. Aunt Mary Bunker, wife of the
Bishop, was the acting mid-wife of the town.
She came the customary ten days to bathe the
baby while I was in bed. We called him Reuben
LeRoy. As soon as his father learned of the
birth, he came down to Bunkerville. I have
never had a doctor at the birth of any of my
children, nor at any other time for that matter,
and I have never paid more than five dollars
for the services of a mid-wife.

When my baby was just a year old, my
brother Christian came down on horseback to
tell me that mother had died of la grippe. To
make a light conveyance, we took the running-
gears of a wagon, laid boards across, and
padded them with hay and quilts to soften
the jolts. Then with my youngest children and
with Albert for a driver, we left home at four
o'clock in the morning. We arrived at Beaver
Dams at sun-up, took fresh horses that my son-

in-law-to-be, Henry Leavitt, had taken ahead, and hurried on to Santa Clara by eight that night. The next morning the funeral was held.

Afterwards we divided Mother's belongings into four piles, then drew cuts to see which should belong to each of us four children. In the draw I got Mother's bedstead that she had slept on all these years; and some of her nice dishes. We each got seventy-five dollars from money left her by a relative in Switzerland.

It pained me to see that father was fast losing his eyesight. Ever since he had been caught in a blizzard years before, his eyes had troubled him. Often they were sore and inflamed, and now within a year he was to go totally blind, and to be so the fifteen remaining years of his life. He had always been such a hard worker that the handicap of blindness was very hard on him. He would sometimes cry like a child because he was unable to do much work. But he did a good deal, even though blind. He would feel his way with a stick across the wide ditch and into his lot, where he would cut lucern and carry it to his cows. Once he came down to Bunkerville and stayed with me for a while.

With the $75 received at mother's death, I bought some store goods, brought them to

Bunkerville, and sold them off and on for the next two years, thinking I could make a little money in that way. Finally I gave up that venture because it tied me too close. Besides, I did not make much profit, and goods let out on credit were not always paid for, especially those sold to Indians.

I did not want to be a burden on my husband, but tried with my family to be self-supporting. I picked cotton on shares to add to our income; would take my baby to the fields while the other children were at school, for I never took the children out of school if it could possibly be avoided. That cotton picking was very tiresome, back-breaking work but it helped to clothe my children.

I always kept a garden so we could have green things to eat. Keeping that free from weeds and watering it twice a week took lots of time. With a couple of pigs, a cow, and some chickens, we got along pretty well.

In the spring of the year, when the grass sprang up on the hills, almost everybody turned their cows out to graze for the day. Sometimes they failed to return at night, unless there was a young calf to call them back. Often I have walked almost to the mountains, to hunt for and bring back the straying cows. We had alfalfa, or lucern as we called it, in the lot and the children or I always cut it with a sickle or scythe throughout the summer to feed the cows. In the early spring, before the lucern was high enough to cut, we would go to the field and fill sacks with young sweet clover and bring it home to the cows. This clover or young lucern we would mix with straw so the cows would not bloat on it.

We made good use of the grapes on the lot. The thinskins we dried into raisins on the roof of the kitchen. I always made some batches of jam, usually out of the Californias. The Lady Downings and tough-skins we usually sent fresh with peddlers to the mining camps. Albert frequently took them to Delamar or Pioche.

The year after mother died, my oldest girl married—September 3, 1895. She was only seventeen and I hated to see her go, but she got a good husband and has raised a fine family since.

In the spring of 1896 I took my three youngest children and went up to the March conference. Now that Mother was dead, I always stayed with my sister Rosie whenever I visited Santa Clara. When I walked in with

my babies there lay Ella, Rosie's little girl, all
blotched with red measles.

A week after I got back home with my
family they all broke out with measles. One
night when I was weary from caring for the
sick children, I fell asleep on top of the bed.
My boy Wilford, eight years old, crawled out
of bed and took a big drink of cold water. The
measles went in on him and do what we would
we were unable to help him. Smothering spells
came on and he jumped up fighting for breath.
Shortly before he died he kept looking up to
the corner of the ceiling and saying, "I'm coming." And then he left us. I felt somewhat reconciled to his going because of the dream I
had had when he was a baby. I believed that
his time had come; that God wanted him on
the other side.

For years I had longed for a cool cellar
and for a kitchen built onto the house. Albert
went out to Mount Trumbell and worked for
lumber. He chopped trees for a while and then
returned with a load of lumber to build the
kitchen for us. His father helped dig the cellar
and lay up the walls with rock. Then they
made a trip to the nearby mountain and got
some heavy cedar and pine logs to put over the
cellar. These served as joists below the kitchen

floor. Adobe walls for a nice big room were laid up and a roof topped them. But the rooms could not be finished until we had more lumber. Again Albert drove a hundred miles to the Trumbell saw mill and worked for another load. The room was finally finished and we surely welcomed the new comfort of more space.

By this time I had become a grandmother. Mary had a fine little baby girl. But it lived only to be a year and a half old and then died. Mary took sick over the strain and was bedfast for six weeks, but she pulled through all right.

In the spring of 1900 Albert decided to marry. He had been my mainstay for a good part of his life but he was now twenty-six years old and it was time for him to head a family of his own. Even after he was married he was very good to me; kept up the farm and did all he could. For a year he and Ellen, his wife, lived with us. Then his father gave him a lot and part of the farm for himself.

In December of the year when Albert married, Bertha, my second daughter, also wed. One by one my children were leaving the home roof to make homes of their own. Conditions were gradually getting better and living was a

MARY ANN HAFEN AND CHILDREN IN 1907

Standing, left to right: Bertha, Mary, Selena.
Sitting: LeRoy R., Mary Ann, Lovena.
Insert: Albert (taken while in Switzerland).

little easier for us all. Throughout the hard years I had managed to keep my children in school, and they had about as good an education as they could get here at home. For two years Selena went off to high school; then came home to teach school for a year, but married before the winter was through (December 23, 1902).

Before Albert's second boy was born, Albert was called on a mission to Germany. I had always looked forward to this day when my son could go forth as a missionary for the church.

In 1909 Lovena married, and Roy was the only one left. Before long, however, he went away winters to school, and I was left alone. In the quiet evenings I used to sit and think— and still do—of the times when my children were all at home and everything was so lively.

The children all liked music. All the girls learned to play the guitar and Albert and Roy learned to play the violin. We wanted so much to have an organ, but never could afford one. Our house had for years been a gathering place for the young people of the town. Almost every Sunday night they would gather around our front doorstep and sing songs while one of my girls played accompaniment on the guitar. Albert and later Roy also played the violin for the town dances and sometimes one of the girls played accompaniment on the town organ. This being left alone was very hard to bear.

But it wasn't long before grandchildren began to come to the house. They especially liked to come when the mulberries and later when the grapes were ripe. And it was a pleasure to be able to give them something they liked.

All my children except one have settled down in Bunkerville or in Mesquite (five miles away, across the river), so I should not complain, for I can see them often and visit with them.

The year before Roy finished college he married—on September 3, 1915, twenty years to the day from the time that my first daughter, Mary, was married. After completing college at Brigham Young University, Roy brought his wife and baby to live with me while he taught in the Bunkerville high school. At the beginning of his third year he was made Principal of the school. The next year I tended his babies, Karl and Norma while his wife taught with him. It seemed good to have children in my home again.

One summer we built a cistern, which was quite an improvement over the old drinking barrel of water which we used to dip up from the running ditch. It cost about ninety dollars besides the work. Albert, Roy, and Edgar Leavitt laid it up. I still enjoy the fresh cool water from it. We always try to fill it in the spring when the snow water comes down in flood. Then the water is much softer than the river water is at ordinary times.

In 1920 Roy took his family and me on a trip to Salt Lake City in his new Ford car. It was my first visit there since my marriage, forty-five years before. The temple which now stood up so beautifully with its stately spires had been but a mass of stones, with workmen pounding and chiseling, when I was there so many years ago.

Then Roy took his family and moved to Berkeley, California. He wanted to continue his education. Already he had taken out his Master's degree from the University of Utah by attending summer schools and had written a thesis on the Handcart Migration to Utah. But he still wanted to go higher.

Once again I was alone in my home. During the next few years I rented my house and lot and went to St. George where I could work in the temple.

While Roy was still at Berkeley I took a trip to California to visit him. It was lovely there by the ocean, and seeing all the beauties of the coast. The next year he took his degree —Doctor of Philosophy—and then got the position of Historian in Denver, Colorado.

My husband, who was still living in Santa Clara, died on May 4, 1928, in his ninetieth year. In recent years he had seldom come down to Bunkerville to see us. In the first years, when we were getting started down here, he came frequently and helped us a good deal. But afterwards he had his hands full taking care of his other families.

My children and I went up to the funeral. He had been living with Anna, his third wife. His first and his fourth wives had passed on before he did, my sister Rosie in 1912 and Susette in 1914.

He was a good man, reared fine children, and did the best he could by us all. His grandson, Arthur K. Hafen, published a sketch of his life in 1929, in which were listed all his descendants. They totaled 211—27 children, 131 grandchildren, and 53 great-grandchildren

JOHN G. HAFEN AND GRANDCHILDREN,
KARL AND NORMA HAFEN, IN 1924

on his eighty-ninth birthday, October 17, 1927.

Polygamy was hard to live, both for the man and the women. But we went into it in obedience to the Lord's command and strived to subdue our jealous feelings and live in accord with the spirit of the Gospel of Jesus Christ. Some time before his death, John said, "I complied with the celestial law of plural marriage in obedience to the Church authorities and because the command was divinely inspired. It cost me much heartache and sorrow and I have shed many tears over it. But I feel that the sacrifices I made have brought great blessings, and I am satisfied."

In recent years I have enjoyed working in the St. George temple. I am so happy to be able to do good in this way. I have found no other work that gives me so much satisfaction now that my children are grown and have families of their own.

In my Patriarchal Blessing I was promised that I should have comforting dreams to cheer and bless me in times of need. And this has surely come true.

I had an interesting experience the winter of 1928, when I was living in St. George. My granddaughter Pansy came up to stay with me during her confinement. I was not feeling very well, as the flu had left me with a bad cough, but I tried to take care of her. We slept in the same bed. One morning I woke up sobbing. Pansy asked me what was the matter. At first I could not answer her, I was so overcome with joy. Then I told her I had seen the Saviour in His glorified body and smiling face. It seemed to be more than a dream, a sort of vision. It was such a comfort to me and will be as long as I live.

Some time ago I had a sweet dream. I found myself in a large assembly gathered for Sabbath worship. A large choir of singers were on the stage. In the first song the soprano led with a most beautiful, clear voice and the rest followed in a sort of chant, all the parts blending so beautifully. The second song was in march time and was sung with such vigor and enthusiasm that it seemed to shake the whole house, and a light cloud hovered over the singers and I felt that I was in heaven. Then they all moved away in a group, piano and all, singing as they went. Even when I woke it seemed to sound in my ears and I felt to thank the Lord for the beautiful thing I had seen and heard.

In 1931 Roy invited me to visit him and his family in Denver. I started on June 15th with my grandson Melvin Leavitt for Logan, Utah. We stopped over night with my grandson Laurel Leavitt at Provo, then went on to Logan and met my brother John. We were so glad to see each other again. I stayed with him and his family until the 23d, then went to Salt Lake City and we went through the Temple one day and stayed with his son William Stucki in Salt Lake. They all treated me with great kindness.

Then I went to Denver on the train. Roy and his family were all well and I enjoyed a good visit with them for two months. They took me on trips through the beautiful mountains, over wonderful, paved roads, by lakes and streams and through great groves of trees covering the mountain sides. I enjoyed the city parks, museums and other attractions. I appreciated their kindness to me very much.

On May 5, 1935, all my children and most of my grandchildren and their children came to my home to give me a birthday party. Roy and his wife drove from Denver to join with the others. They all brought picnic and we had such an enjoyable time. The many children made the place ring with their shouts and laughter. The big mulberry trees furnished shade for all. At night they played the guitar and sang songs as they used to.

The next day Roy and Ann took me down to Las Vegas and out to the Boulder dam. The water was already backed up some miles above the giant cement dam. We took a ride on the lake in a motor boat and sped over the water with the spray sprinkling our faces. It was so thrilling. We rode up to the base of the big dam, which towered several hundred feet above us, although the water was already over a hundred feet deep beneath us. Then we drove around to the top of the dam and saw the men working to finish it, with big steel cables stretched across the great canyon and the marvelous machinery at work dumping cement and doing such work. I stayed over night with my granddaughter Pansy Hardy at Las Vegas and enjoyed the visit with her.

I was honored at three special birthday parties in May, 1938. On May 4th, the day before my birthday, one of the school teachers, Mrs. Alton Peterson, entertained all the women of the town at a social in my honor. She made a cake with eighty-four candles on it and we spent a very pleasant afternoon.

On my birthday, all the members of my family except Roy and wife, who are in Denver, were at my home for the afternoon. They all brought lunch and we enjoyed ourselves in the shade of the trees.

On "Mother's Day," May 8th, I was again honored at a special program in Sunday School and in Church. The Bishopric and members of the Relief Society had planned it and thought that it would be appropriate for members of my family to prepare the program, which pleased me very much. The Singing Mothers (a group of Relief Society members) sang three beautiful numbers. Bishop Donald Tobler made the opening remarks. After this a group of about twenty little grandchildren marched up to where I sat and sang, "Happy Birthday to You, Dear Grandma," when two of them, Nita Rae and Elaine, placed on my head a wreath of roses that had been prepared by Sisters Annie E. Cox and Luella Leavitt. I was embarrassed and felt that they were doing more than I was worthy of. The rest of the program was rendered by my children and in-laws, after which members in the audience asked if they might say a few words. Brothers Harmon Tobler and Thomas Adams each told of incidents in their lives when I had been of assistance to them in times of trouble, but which I had entirely forgotten. All in all it was a very pleasant occasion and I felt that I had many friends.

For a long time I had wanted to make another visit to Denver to see my son Roy and family, but as I was failing in health somewhat I hardly dared undertake the trip alone. So I asked my daughter Mary to accompany me, which she gladly did. We left home on August 2nd with Warren Hardy, who came and offered to take us as far as Cedar City, where we took the train for Denver. We found Roy and family well and happy to see us and we were royally treated while at their home. They took us on a trip to the mountains and to many places of interest in the city. We were especially pleased to visit the State Museum, where he is in charge, and to see the many historical exhibits and beautiful models on display there. His library of Western books, the *Colorado Magazine* which he edits, and the historical volumes he has written were very interesting to us. The reading of his latest book, *Fort Laramie and the Pageant of the West*, gave me great pleasure and stirred many memories, for it deals with the trail I followed so many years ago.

I have not done much in the way of public office, but have tried to do my best whenever

called upon.   Back in 1873 I was chosen as
first councilor to Anna Ensign in the Santa
Clara Relief Society.   After we had moved to
Bunkerville I served as second councilor to
Anna Barnum in the Relief Society.   After my
release in 1906, I served as a teacher in the
Relief Society.   When Harriet Earl was President of the Primary I was a teacher in this or-
ganization for several years.

In recent years I have spent as much time
as possible in Temple work, and have great joy
in doing good in this way.   I have done the
work for about 1,500 names and have made
some money donations for the work.

My father Samuel Stucki was a hard working man.   He worked from daylight till dark,
on the farm or in his workshop.   He was liberal
hearted and always willing to share his meager
means.   I remember one time a neighbor came
for flour when we had only a small amount ourselves, but he gave them some.   Mother scolded
him and said he would give the last we had in
the house if someone else needed it.   He was
very religious, always paid an honest tithing
and was strict in honoring the Sabbath and
attending meetings.   He chided us when we
wanted to get a good dinner on Sunday.   He
said for us to make some cake or pie on Satur-

day so we could just have a cold lunch on Sunday.

My mother was also very religious. I remember how she used to have us children sit down at her knees and tell us the stories of the Bible and bring us to tears telling about the life and the crucifixion of our dear Saviour.

My parents left a comfortable home and surroundings for the Gospel's sake and came out into a wilderness and endured every hardship in obedience to the call of God. I hope and pray that my offspring may honor them and walk in the paths of righteousness.

I thank the Lord for my dear children that He has blessed me with and for the wisdom and light they have to become useful in His hands to help carry on His work on the earth. They are now rearing fine families of their own. The Lord has been good to care for us all in time of need and protect us from danger. I am thankful for his many blessings and hope that my offspring will live true and upright lives and be good examples to their children and associates, that they will keep faith in God and live in obedience to his Gospel, for I know that eternal life is the reward of the faithful.

I want to bear my testimony that God lives and that he answers prayers. He has healed me and mine in time of sickness and comforted us in days of distress and sorrow. He is ever ready to listen to a prayer from the heart. He has a watchful eye over us, if only we will trust Him, walk humbly, and keep His commandments.

The Lord has given us the Gospel through his Son Jesus Christ and that should mean more to us than anything else in this life. If anything I have done or written here will influence some one to do good I shall be happy and thankful. For it is by our works that we gain salvation and this life is but a stepping stone to a higher life that is worth every effort and sacrifice that we can make.

The truths of the Gospel are ground deep in my soul. God lives to reward our good works and His Gospel is the true way to Life and salvation. This life is short and when we die we can take nothing with us but our good works. If we live faithful in this life we can go on in the next and have eternal progression in the Kingdom of God.

I have tried to acknowledge the hand of the Lord in all things. Trials and difficulties of all kinds often turn out for our own good in the long run. The Lord knows better than we do what is best for us and we should humbly bow to his will.

May the Lord bless us all and keep us true to Him. I hope and trust that my children, grandchildren and their children will ever turn to Him in the hour of trouble and they will surely find strength. May they love the Lord with all their might, mind and strength and their neighbors as themselves. Then the blessing of happiness and the joy that passeth understanding will be their reward. And we shall all meet again in a holier sphere and be re-united in the presence of our Lord and Saviour Jesus Christ.

I pray the Lord to bless you and guard you. May His spirit be ever with you to guide and comfort you through life, that you may walk in obedience to his laws and commandments and gain salvation and life eternal in His presence, is the humble prayer of your loving mother, Mary Ann Hafen.